MACHINE LEARNING IN PYTHON

Hands on Machine Learning with Python Tools, Concepts and Techniques

Disclaimer

Table of Contents

Finally, We Come to A Close

Machine Learning with Python is Not Easy

Machine Learning with Python is Easy

What is Machine Learning?

How Programming Normally Works

The usual method of programming is quite linear, even in places where it seems non linear. The most common "insult" that some programmers use to refer to machine learning is that it is just a bunch of if… else statements where the machine is not actually learning. It is very easy to understand how these programmers come to understand this, but it is important to realize that they are only half right.

Let's look at how something like a website and Photoshop works, considering how widely the manner in which they operate is different. A website is a collection of HTML, CSS, and Javascript with whatever backend code implementation they plan to use. The website itself does not normally install anything on the user desktop and utilizes features that are already there.

The only mechanism that provides change is the web browser itself and it is only when the web browser supports changes in those languages do those languages *really* have access to new features. In order to construct the front-end of the website, one has to load the HTML, which will then load the CSS in the Head or the Body areas of the page and load the Javascript in, usually, the Body area of the page near the footer. Therefore, it is linearly loaded no matter how interconnected the web pages may seem.

In Photoshop, the implementation is definitely different due to the fact that it is a program that must be installed on a computer. To the average individual, Photoshop looks like a self-contained unit that can be utilized on every platform. However, Photoshop must utilize and have access to graphical standards only found in drivers for Graphics Cards. In order to draw a line, Photoshop normally has to make a call to the Direct X 11 or Direct X 12 or Vulkan or OpenGL libraries. No one really knows which library it calls to or if it calls to all of them, but all graphics-based programs have to call on existing libraries. This doesn't become apparent until the program encounters an error.

You might ask how I know this and it really has to deal with the variation of Graphics Cards on the market. You have Intel, AMD, and NVidia all making their own versions of Graphics Chips, with each version of these chips running on the previously mentioned libraries and even older ones. With AMD alone, I know that the past 10 years have seen Direct X 9, Direct X 10, Direct X 11, and Vulkan chip libraries. These libraries provide a consistent basis for function calls across the variety of Graphics Chips in the market. It would be impractical for Adobe, developers of Photoshop, to create their software from complete scratch for each Graphics Chip in existence when there are pre-existing libraries that other companies maintain that cut the workload significantly.

Therefore, in order for a program like Photoshop to even work, it has to have a linear access to already implemented resources. Photoshop, itself, is very modular but still linear. You can see this in how it structures its' menus. I click on Filter to find the Blur category where I can use the Gaussian Blur equation. Photoshop can be seen more like a library of different image related equations that have sub-equations to ultimately create a linear stack of *Layers* as they are referred to in Photoshop. Therefore, while the tools are modular, they are nested linearly and applied to the image in a chronologically linear methodology.

Having this in mind and having seen programs and websites work like this for decades, it is understandable that Machine Learning could be seen as nothing more than if... else statements. The problem doesn't rely on how programming works, but rather on how if... else statements are seen. For instance, *if true then this else then that* is a valid way to teach new programmers how to understand if... else statements. The programmers who compare Machine Learning to this could say *if (feature has curve) then feature is a, b, c... else feature is L, A, E...* and this could very well be a valid representation of how a network might work. However, that is how the human mind works and we learn all the time so what's the problem?

How We Define Learning

The problem, therefore, is the definition of what it means to learn, and this is indeed a philosophical discussion. You might have been asking why I have laid this out in such a manner, but it is truly important to understand that machine learning works differently than the average programming as it has been practiced. It is different not because of *how* it is programmed, but with what *intent* it is programmed for. This is why the philosophy is also important as it determines how one goes about making and implementing machine learning.

How does the human mind learn? It learns through practicing until it gets *it* mostly right. Therefore, our recognition usually fails us the first few times that we attempt to apply it. It is only through repeated failure that *human minds* find their Gradient Descent. Gradient Descent is how Machine Learning works, but exactly what is it? It is a mathematical equation given to us by Calculus and while it has many applications, Machine Learning uses it to measure the amount of error an algorithm has and move towards less error.

The philosophy behind Machine Learning is to define how *human minds* would normally classify Features mathematically at their most fundamental levels. Once we have this definition, we then begin to write algorithms that are designed to find these features in a more general sense because we humans don't make things with perfection as it would be in a computer world. For instance, while a circle is a circle in the human world it will eventually boil down into a line if we zoom in close enough. The computational world views it from a mathematical equation, which means it will never become a line no matter how much we zoom into it. Once we have written the drafts of these programs, these *if... else statements*, we begin to repeatedly test them to see how accurate they are when applied. This produces an error rate with each test and the goal is to make the error rate drop via a Gradient Descent.

In Calculus, this Gradient Descent is really just an X and Y plot line that curves with hills and valleys. The goal for those developing the Machine Learning algorithms is to create an error rate that exists inside of the lowest possible valley. Each error rate represents a plot point. However, this is still very much a Linear Program because we make it, test it, and change it to make it *more* correct and this doesn't constitute as learning. Learning requires that an algorithm is able to review past mistakes, use those mistakes to get better results, and make fewer mistakes. Thus, the key to unlocking a Learning Algorithm is how one can make the algorithm *remember and change* its' algorithm for better results.

The Cleverness of Recursive Programming

When looking at Machine Learning programs, the most common theme you will see is that those programmers will often run these programs thousands of times to see what it does. While we could very well explain the different methodologies behind how one goes about teaching an algorithm, the most important facet is that the programmer is looking for the correct weights and biases to get the best Gradient Descent. Here, I am going to discuss one of the many types of algorithms used that will help you understand why most programmers make their programs recursive.

Let us say that we have a dataset of 100 randomized characters and we want our algorithm to recognize letters. The first method is where we have Supervised Learning, which is where we know the correct answer for every character that goes into our Machine Learning algorithm. The goal here would be to feed the character through the algorithm, see if it guessed correctly, and change values if it got it wrong. We could do this by hand, but this is usually time-consuming and human error prone, like reusing values by accident. When it comes to individual feature detection, this is manageable. You may only have to test 100 times for each feature to make sure it detects the fundamentals.

However, when you have to detect if the Machine Learning algorithm can utilize those feature detection nodes in unison, it becomes a mathematical nightmare to do it by hand. Basically, you can think of it as a factorial equation with each feature detection node adding one more to the factorial. Therefore, if you are testing for seven features, you would need to test it by hand seven factorial or 5,040 times. Instead, we would be much better off if we had the program detect when it was wrong, have it change its' own values, and then reattempt to guess correctly. This, by definition, is a recursive algorithm, which is the most common way Machine Learning is practiced. However, having a known database with known values is still Supervised Learning regardless of whether it is recursive or not, recursion just makes the process faster.

The importance of recursion inside of Machine Learning cannot be understated because this is how the algorithm teaches itself from then on. Imagine having to correct every error Google Voice

Recognition provided by hand; it's simply impossible for one human. Thus, recursion allows the programmer to run test batches via Supervised or Unsupervised and glean information on whether it is working well or something needs to be changed in the fundamentals. While I may not have defined all of the points, this is generally how Machine Learning works and is applied.

The Core of ML is Feature Detection

Now, I have talked a lot about Feature Detection without actually defining what it is and this is because it is an abstract concept rather than a defined item. For instance, when you look at the letter A, it will have different features to it than the letter a. Instead of looking for a direct definition, you would look for features like a straight line or a curve in the letter to determine parts of a whole. Parts of a whole is a great way to think about how Feature Detection works because that is how *all* Machine Learning algorithms sift through the data.

In order to create a feature, you have to Classify or Categorize those features that you define. The entirety of creating features is ultimately to determine "what does it mean?" because what does it mean if the letter has a curve? The natural answer would mean that it could only be part of a smaller set of structures. Let us go through the process of *detecting* or *recognizing* "Creek". Right off the bat we have something unique; the "C" is bigger than the other letters, which means it is capitalized. We could run a matrix to determine the size of all the individual characters. This would take the total amount of letters it could be down to 26, effectively cutting the search size down by half. Then we could notice that it has a curve, which would likely cut it down to just 10 of those letters. Now we could notice it is an open circle, which further cuts it down to G and C. Lastly, we could notice that it doesn't have a line in the middle, which gives us a guess of C. We would then follow a similar process for each of the characters in the string.

The important part to notice is that the Features we created were from noticeable differences in the data. Additionally, each "notice" was applicable to every letter we tried to recognize, which meant we could reuse those feature detection tools. This is how you create Features from what seems like random data no matter what algorithm you might be using at the time, but you really only have to start out with one feature and then it becomes much easier to define even more features.

The Development of "Neural Nodes"

As I have related to in the past, we in Machine Learning often reference our ideas about Machine Learning from how our *human mind* works. This is because the mind is the one reference point we can most relate to and the scientific basis for which we already have a significant scientific background (Psychology, Anatomy, ect..). This allows us to theorize how we might make a machine capable of the same *useful* mechanisms we have as humans.

The research essentially boiled down to what we know as the Perceptron, which is the first type of neural network ever to be conceived of and implemented successfully.

```
function node(x){
    if(weight * x + bias > 0){
        return 1;
    }else{
        return 0;
    }
}
```

The Perceptron is binary classifier that uses the code above as a basis of its' equation (yes, the real version is a bit more complicated) and it is the simplest example of what we call a neural node. Now, for the longest time, the weights and bias referred in this algorithm constantly confused me as to what they associate themselves to. Here is the equation for Slope Intercept Form:

$$y = mx + b$$

In Slope Intercept Form, we are trying to find where a singular point intercepts the slope of a line. In a Binary Classifier, we are attempting to classify if a singular point is before or after a slope. In the case of the program we utilized, we are simply detecting if the classified value is above or below zero. You probably already noticed how the Slope Intercept Form is very similar to that of the Binary classifier, which was how I actually understood weights and biases for the first time.

In Slope Intercept Form, the m is where we obtain our slope, the b is our Y intercept, and our x is just our x plot point. Therefore, our weight is how we define what the slope is and then the bias is really our

Y intercept. Instead of equalizing it to Y, we simply determine if the result is below Y or above Y. Normally, the weights are actually randomized because all we have is data and we're trying to find the correlation between 0 and 1. The value of b is determined by how far off the slope is supposed to be from 0. Needless to say, that I am simplifying this far further than most academic papers might, but this is how it works in the most basic sense.

Once we have our neuron up and running, we now need to make it into a node and this is what we need the Activation Function for. There are several different Activation Functions out there and our basis of the Perceptron does have its' own activation by either returning a 1 or a 0 otherwise known as Binary Activation. The Activation Function is used to determine if it is going to send a value to the next node in the network or not, which actually makes itself a neural node rather than a neuron.

Finally, what is Machine Learning?

While I might have delved a little bit into the Perceptron, it is only a single example in the library of different neurons utilized in a neural network. In this chapter, we have covered the misguided notion that machine learning is just a bunch of if… else statements and we have also gone over what actually makes up a neural network, but now it is time to finally answer the question of "What is Machine Learning?" and there's a couple answers to the question depending on how you approach it.

The definition of machine learning is the ability for a machine to make decisions based on data and then based on the outcomes of those decisions, change how it works so that it is capable of making better decisions. For instance, let's go through a logic tree.

- Is this a Box? -

    -> Does box have vertical lines?

- Yes

    -> Does box have horizontal lines?

- Yes

    -> Does each horizontal line vector with a vertical line?

- Yes

    -> Box prediction

- Yes

    Answer = No

In such a situation, the questions asked of the neural network about an item may suggest that it is a box, but it could also just be four corners that don't interconnect with each corner. The answers would be right, but there's no room for self-correction and the logic tree is incomplete. This would be a machine learning algorithm if we simply added better questions, which is why neural networks are usually quite large.

The other definition of machine learning is that it is the ability for a machine to remember incorrect predictions and correct predictions, which through the comparison of those memories that the machine makes more correct predictions. However, you run into the definition problem with this and so the application of machine learning algorithm becomes societally based. For instance, how do we determine if another human is an enemy? If you answered that they must have caused us harm, then we could say every human is an enemy because they take usable air away from us so they can live.

The last definition and perhaps the more preferred is that machine learning is an algorithm designed to provide estimated predictions based on mathematical classifications and datasets. This allows machine learning to be an abstract construct that is defined by the application it is used in. These are the primary answers to a seemingly simple yet complex question, which really represents the potential complexity and difficulty of machine learning.

Why use Python?

Python is Quick to Pick Up

Python is an extremely easy language to pick up and was originally designed to be easy to pick up. The knowledge of how Python works was originally based on work the creator had performed in ABC with interpreted languages. Very much like how many of the languages that were developed at the time, Guido van Rossum had issues with how the languages he worked on actually worked. One Christmas, he decided to write Python and he so named it after Monty Python's Flying Circus.

Alright, so it wasn't specifically built for ease of use, which is Ruby's claim to fame. Instead, the developer of the language saw the need to have an easy interface to low level items. However, historically, Python is usually the introductory programming languages for those not going into Computer Science as a way to convince them that programming is not difficult.

Python is an interpreted language, which means that you don't need to waste time making definitions for items that should be quite obvious. With languages like C++ and Java, the benefit to having control over the definitions primarily has to deal with memory management and speed. Since Python is an interpreted language, many see a very drastic decrease in speed, but most don't notice that there are other arguments in play. Most Machine Learning is *done* with Python, but when it is put into production the odds of the program being translated to a language like C, like C++, or like Java are very high. This is because Python is very good at allowing developers to refine the mechanics without having to wield a foray of definition errors off with a cyber stick.

Not only does this cut down on time but it also allows users to pick up the language very quickly. Those familiar with programming and diving into Machine Learning can utilize background knowledge to easily jump into Python without much trouble. Most anyone who has a background in data analysis or manipulation can jump into Python because of how important Matlab is to the data analytical world. Matlab is an all-encompassing mathematical library that helps those manipulating data to create graphs and since Python can manipulate Excel, the other Math Lord software, Python is kind of a programming math king language. Due to the nomenclature of Python, those sufficiently studied in mathematics will easily transition into programming because almost all of the syntax is math-based. Pretty much, if you're doing something with math and it involves programming, Python is your heavyweight champion.

This implies that Python is really easy to pick up if you're naturally inclined to be a mathematician regardless of level, which is primarily true of most programming. However, it's also not just the mathematical side that benefits Python but also Blender, The Sims 4 and Eve Online. These are very well-known programs that harness the power of Python, but Blender in particular does a really good job because a sufficient enough Blender user can use Python in Blender. You might be wondering why I bring up these three, specific software applications of Python to the forefront.

Blender is a 3D Graphics Modelling and Animation software, which is vastly popular due to the fact that it has been free and will seemingly remain free. There are hundreds of thousands of tutorials on YouTube and ever more on the internet about how to use Blender. With the widespread popularity of the program, it is only natural that when you become an advanced user of Blender that you begin to use the Python console. By using this console, it is like unlocking an entirely different version of Blender where a lot more can be done.

As for Eve Online and The Sims 4, these are massive video games that have culturally affected every country they have been in. Video games, in my opinion, is a huge reason why younger generations show interest in learning how to program. In the beginning adventures of many programmers, a primary question is "what the most popular video game language is" so that those programmers can learn the language to create games. Those who are a fan of Civilizations and Eve Online tend to profess Python because it is used extensively between the two. Eve Online, though, is popular because of its' cultural impact and so is The Sims 4.

In Eve Online, it has been debated as whether the crime committed in the game constitutes as actual crime in the real world.

This is because there have been several controversial incidents where users scam, pirate, and induce corporate espionage in the virtual game. The developers purposely refuse to do anything about it and enforce the idea that players should not sink money into the game for items if they're not prepared to lose it. The organization controlling the game actually created an internal affairs segment to ensure the developers did not take advantage of their position, back in a time when computer-based organizations hadn't commonly thought this to be a standard practice. There are wars inside cyberspace that result in huge "wartime" losses in a way never seen before. There was a 6,142-player war that eventually came to be known as the Siege of 9-4 that cost over one million dollars in real currency.

There is a subculture in Eve Online that produces mods to allow the game to be operated and to operate in a much more organized manner. These mods have to be written in the same language as the original product in order to avoid compatibility issues both online and offline. While the User Interface is offline, much of the data that is utilized in Eve Online mods rely on what is coming in through the connection, so it needs to handle specific Python data typing.

YouTube is the primary reason why The Sims 4 became so popular because it was a center of attention for many massive YouTubers such as DanTDM, Pewdiepie, and others. It was part of the meme culture and unlike Blender or Eve Online, it didn't hold much importance beyond that. With older games though, the code is usually much easier to break because people found vulnerabilities in it. Additionally, it also helps if that same code either has poor encryption or no encryption, which is where the modding community for Python comes in again. As I explained with Eve Online, in order to mod a game and prevent compatibility issues, the mod usually uses the same language that was used to make the game. With over 500 mods in the Sims 4 community, a game that is quite old by our standards has a very active modding community.

This means that a lot of modders for these two games and more wind up using Python as a result. Therefore, subcultures of the genre would naturally be swayed to hold Python above other languages. Add in the likelihood that these subcultures could pick up on Python quickly and you have a fanbase spawned entirely from other areas of the economic tree for entirely different reasons. This leads into the next reason why Machine Learning is Python-Popular.

Python has a Massive Science and Community-Based Culture

You might be asking why I chose these three specific software products to explain why Python is quick to pick up because you do not see a correlation between those products and machine learning. They do have a correlation and that is in the amount of data that's utilized. For Blender, this community focuses on graphical standards and making much of what we see in games, animated movies, and the list goes on. There's a massive amount of geometrical and geospatial data in Blender. Eve Online is an economic system with a massive player base powering it, which means that there's a ton of data passing through the mods and being displayed for players. Sims 4 has to deal with an emotional setting where player interactions with non-player entities result in emotional and financial consequences in the game. All three products utilize and harness massive quantities.

However, at the same time that they utilize massive quantities they are also very simplistic in the needs that are met. For instance, in

Blender you may just want to automate a specific skeleton that would be a slight variation of the original. A mutant may have six or four fingers, teeth, a few teeth or all teeth, and at this point you can think of this like a game like Spore. Instead of spending hundreds of hours trying to create all the different variations, one can simply write a clever Python script that will take the base model and modify it. In order to do this, a person has to be a competent person in several difficult mathematical fields.

In the Eve Online modding community, some of the more basic mods are simply creating User Interface mechanisms that list team player statistics, player locations, and even financial charts like one would see in a Wall Street office. This level of mathematics is more about knowing Statistics 101 and beyond with a little bit of Predictive Analysis to help control the flows of the market. When everybody is trying to gain with the same math, it becomes a mathematical war among players.

In Sims 4, most of the mods are either visual or psychological, which requires an understanding of two different fields. Those that are visual not only require the knowledge of reverse engineering but also the same level of mathematics needed in Blender Python. Those that are psychological have to know Community Economics, Ecosystem Analysis, and other fields in order to make a mod that doesn't break the game by making it impossible to win or taking away from the purpose of the main game.

Python is a language that sort of specializes in all of these types of mathematics. While the main language has a heavy amount of support for code libraries like OpenCV, Matlab's, PyChart, and similar mathematically based code libraries, the modding communities provide a different set of resources. Machine learning or neural networks has really been focused on how to utilize machines to better benefit people and companies. Text-based recognition networks are designed to take literary texts and translate them into digital words much faster than humans can. Predictive networks have been helping to create safer trafficking systems on the streets, safer security measures in highly sensitive spots, and even help try and game the economic gambling market. Image recognition has been tested for recognizing medical diseases better and faster than doctors, recognizing faces in crowded zones, and another level of conspiratorial purposes as shown by Hollywood. Any mathematics using image recognition needs to rely on the same mathematical skills Blender programmers use. Predictive networks utilize the same types of mathematics in Eve Online and Sims 4. Therefore, you can begin to understand why Machine Learning has begun to take its' place in video games as well, often modifying or replacing existing AI to help challenge players into being better.

Those who study and implement machine learning are usually academic scholars, governmental bodies, corporations, and hobbyists. These are the four primary categories that make up those that are interested in large coding investments like Machine Learning. Most of the information you're going to find is a cross between academic scholars and hobbyists, so it's important to understand where the bulk of your information is coming from. You're not going to get the algorithm that government bodies or corporations use because that's how they make money and control. The academic scholars may have been the ones that created the technology, but the hobbyists made it prosper. It was not the motherboard kit maker that posted forum questions or made StackOverflow, but the hobbyists that used them and shared their issues. The number one thing any programmer will find themselves doing on (practically) a daily basis is looking up a potential solution to an issue they have. These hobbyists created the code libraries and some of the algorithms you'll be using while you study this material. They are the ones who decided how languages work and where they're applied, which is why they often make it easy to understand how they made it. This is the essence of why Python is so easy to pick up. Every one of the groups prefer to get things done in the now rather than later, which is why Python has the syntax that it does.

Python's Syntax Creates Faster Turnaround Times

The art of writing is the most difficult part of novel writing and programming. Not only does the author need to carefully pick the best words to use for the task they're trying to get done, but the language also needs to support those words. Everyone also knows that time is money, so when you combine the two concepts together you get the need to express your ideas quickly to make the most money. This is the primary reason why interpreted languages like JavaScript, Python, PHP, and Ruby exist.

As a result of this, when you are attempting to put an idea into practice then the faster you can create the structure for that idea the faster you can initiate that idea. Since Python users want to have a quick solution, they rely on Python syntax to take care of the nitty, gritty details while they get their idea sorted out. In Python, definition of a function takes this:

```python
def myFunction():
```

Meanwhile, in C++

```cpp
int main(){ return 0; }
```

As you can see, Python does not require that you predict what type of return result that you're going to get while C++ does. This is very important because you may not always know what you want in the idea that you're trying to prosper. Are you going to want an array of coordinates, an integer, or a string of text that your singular function recognized? You haven't even started writing the application and you have to predict what the result will be at the end, which doesn't make a lot of sense. This is why Python syntax is much easier to pick up because the language does not assume you know what you want so it provides a lot more freedom. However, that does not mean that your program is going to stay in the same language.

Python is the Development Language, C is the Production Language

One of the most common practices in programming is the art of translating one program into another program for an advantage. Python syntax may make creating the idea quick, but Python is considerably slow because the program has to interpret that program before it can run that program. As a result, many companies and organizations often take the original program and translate it to C or "bridge it" to C. This takes the step of interpreting the program out of the equation, which drastically reduces the amount of time it takes to execute the program.

As a result, the translated program is usually also the final step in the entire process of making a program. The problem then becomes an issue of whether the functions need to be updated or not. When you work on a program like SolidWorks or Microsoft Word, you make a single program that's going to run the same way unless it is a different version. You can make software that doesn't need constant maintenance, but those ways are actually dying very slowly as many people conform to the idea of the IoT.

The Internet of Things is the idea that all usable items in your house will eventually be connected to the internet. Therefore, imagine that your car registered you are headed home, checks your schedule and sees that you're not going anywhere else. The screen on the dashboard asks if you are headed home and if you want dinner. You then press the "Yes" button on the screen that then tells your fridge, oven, and microwave combo unit to begin making dinner. It then uses the approved container that allows it to remove the lid and puts it into the oven because it's a 30 min dish versus a 30-minute driving route. You walk up to your door, which automatically opens up because it recognizes your IoT key and then closes behind you as it registers you entering and leaving its' scanning region. You are now home with a fresh cooked meal waiting to be pulled out of the oven that you don't need to turn off because the sensors inside the oven tell it to cook it no more as it is now edible.

The problem with the IoT form of life is that it requires the internet and when things are on the internet, actively on the internet like Facebook or StackOverflow, they are almost always never in production. You might find this weird as a concept, but these websites are always developing new features and updating older features. This means, essentially, that they are never truly a final product but rather a series of final products, which would be better known as continued development. So, why is Python important when it comes to an environment of continued development and machine learning?

Python is Web Compatible

Python is often considered to be a "back-end" language. C++ is not considered to be a "back-end" language and C is definitely not a web language. While Python can perform regular software actions, it also has the ability to host web pages and this means that a person can take their machine learning software online. This also means that if your website runs on a different language, you can use what's known as a Python wrapper to create a bridge between your language and the machine learning you're attempting to associate it with, but this is not ideal. You have data transfer rates, Python interpretation, and the program to execute so the cost of running a system like that is unacceptable.

Instead, the most common solution is to just have a Python server that takes the information in and executes the functions like a regular program. This allows your website to function as it normally does and creates an interface where Python can collect the information, send it to the C++ program, and then Python sends it back. It is a necessary cost in most cases because there's not a lot for Python to do other than receive, send, receive back, and then send back. Most of the time is taken up by C++ being executed and the bandwidth involved, which means you don't have to wait long on Python interpretation.

Therefore, if you have a toaster that learns how toasted someone wants their toast to be then you can make a website that the user can control this and other appliances. You can then use this data to make agriculture predictions or sell the information.

So, let's recap, Python is used most often in Machine Learning because:

- It was already popular in Mathematics, Gaming, and Graphic Design culture.

- The syntax makes it fast to develop and prototype.

- The syntax is extremely abstract, which allows an individual to program without needing to predict the result or define everything.

- Due to its' cultural impact, Python has coding libraries and forums that are their own ecosystems, creating massive troves of research and error correction information. This natural backing makes it easier for new programmers to learn the language.

- Finally, Python is already a web capable language, which means that most neural networks (Facial Recognition, Economic Trade Analysis and Prediction, ect.) can easily gather information from the web through Python. Additionally, since a bridge can be made between Python and C++ for a speed advantage, Python is often a first choice for any combination involving analytics and web technologies.

Regression Analysis using Python

What is Regression Analysis?

Now, if you recall, I actually started this book off by comparing the y-intercept formula and Regression Analysis actually utilizes an equation very similar to this.

$$y = \beta_0 + \beta_1 x + \epsilon$$

In this equation, we are saying that the y is equal to that of the y-intercept population parameter plus the slope population parameter plus the error term. The error term is labeled as such because it represents for the unexplained variation in the equation for solving **y**. Essentially, this is the part of the equation we're ultimately trying to reduce so that we can have accurate results. Ultimately, the ideal equation is found below:

$$E(y) = \beta_0 + \beta_1 x$$

The **expected y,** which can also be donated as $\hat{y}$ when working with sample data, is equal to that of the sum of the y-intercept population and slope population parameters. Now, let's back up here because you might not actually understand how to calculate the error term in this equation when you first start out.

Alright, so let's start out by going to the market to negotiate how many trinkets we can buy and for how much. There is no set price for the trinkets and we are buying the same trinket from different sellers. Here is a table that lists 10 sellers and their different price points for selling their trinket to us.

Sellers	Price Points
1	5
2	17
3	11
4	8
5	14
6	20
7	2
8	8
9	11
10	10

In this table, we can see that we have a price point for each of them. Now, can you predict what the next price point will be for the 11th seller in such a graph? Since the only definition we have right now is the price point, the best next prediction will be the mean. The mean is the amount at which there is a 50/50 expectation that it will be the correct prediction. To calculate the mean, we simply add up all the price points and divide them by the number of price points that there are. The mean for this table is 10.6.

Now that we have out mean value, we can now calculate for our residuals. A residual is a number that deviates from the mean value.

While technically all of the values deviate from this, the residual is how much it deviates from the mean. Thus, here is our new table.

Sellers	Price Points	Residuals
1	5	-5.6
2	17	6.4
3	11	0.4
4	8	-2.6
5	14	3.4
6	20	9.4
7	2	-8.6
8	8	-2.6
9	11	0.4
10	10	-0.6

Something to keep in mind here is that the Residuals are the actual Errors we are talking about in Regression Analysis. Now we need to find the **Sum of Squared Errors** or the Sum of Squared Residuals. In the following table, I have done just that.

Residuals	Squared Resid	SSE
-5.6	31.36	260.4
6.4	40.96	
0.4	0.16	
-2.6	6.76	
3.4	11.56	
9.4	88.36	
-8.6	73.96	
-2.6	6.76	
0.4	0.16	
-0.6	0.36	

Now, you might be wondering why we are going through these very specific steps. Simple Linear Regression, the most basic form of Regression Analysis, is based on reducing the SSE (Sum of Squared Errors) to create a **Best Fit Line**. In Linear Regression, we are comparing this SSE that we got when we assumed there was only 1-set of categorizing data (the dependent variable) to another that has 2 sets of categorizing data (the independent and dependent variable). Linear Regression is a part of a special type of mathematics known as Bivariate Statistics. Bivariate means that there are two variables or variations in the Statistics that you may be studying.

In Linear Regression, the Y-Axis is meant to be the "Why?" while the X-Axis is meant to be the "Explanation" of the data. Therefore, "Why is price point 1 at 5?" and then our X-Axis would be used to explain why it is there. You may have also seen that I included a slope in a previous table and that is because the data does have a slope. However, when you are using an equation like this:

$$\hat{y} = b_0 + b_1 x$$

Where the sample data expected y is equal to that of the sample data y-intercept population plus the slope population in order to calculate for 1 variable, you are using a slope of zero. Now we're going to go ahead and add a 2nd variable to our equation, which will be how much money it costs the seller to actually buy the trinket from the person who made it. We will call this new variable the **Initial Cost** as it is the initial cost of the trinket before it is marked up for profit by other sellers. The Price Point is DEPENDENT on the Initial Cost, which a very important distinction to make. Remember that I said that the Y-Axis is the why, thus the Price Point is our new Y plot point and the Initial Cost is our X plot point. Now, here comes a *new* equation:

$$min \sum (y_i - \hat{y}_i)^2$$

This is known as the **Least Squares** equation. If you remember correctly, the **hat of y** is the result we get from our sample data where our Initial Cost didn't exist. The reason why the second y in this equation does not have a hat is because this y is what we will observe of the actual data. The hat of y is our predicted data while the regular y is that actual data. We will be finding the difference of these two, but not on a graph by graph basis. This equation requires us to minimize the sum of the squared differences of each predicted y with each observed y in a linear progression. Here is the new data we will be utilizing:

Sellers	Price Points	Initial Cost
1	5	2.5
2	17	8.5
3	11	5.5
4	8	4
5	14	7
6	20	10
7	2	1
8	8	4
9	11	5.5
10	10	5

I am aware of how clear cut this is, but this is because we're utilizing fake data to make this easier to understand. In the real world, you could spend weeks only to find there's no correlation so for teaching purposes it is much better to have a mock scenario. Instead of looking at this data, you would be putting it in a Scatter Plot like this:

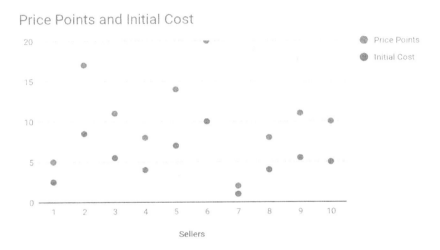

In this graph, it is not as clear that there is a correlation, and this is why data representation is key to seeing the relation between the two. For instance, if I ran this in a Line Graph, the correlation would be glaring:

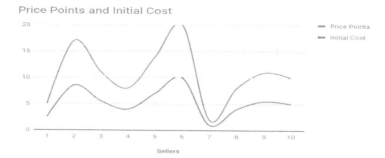

Price Points and Initial Cost

The next step in this process is to find what is known as the **Centroid** and it represents the point at which our Regression Best Fit Line will pass through.

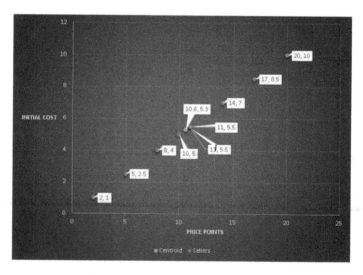

As you can already tell, our Regression Line will most likely go straight through that line. So, the first step in plotting this Regression

Line is to find the Slope or the b_1 of our equation and that equation

requires a bigger equation:

$$\frac{\sum (x_i - \bar{x})(y_i - \bar{y})}{\sum (x_i - \bar{x})^2}$$

Now, this could very well look rather scary at first, but this

equation is actually quite simple. On top, we are finding the difference

between the independent (initial cost) variable as x and the mean of that

independent variable as well as between the dependent variable as y and

the mean of the dependent variable. Then we multiply those together.

Once we are all done doing these to all of the variables, we then add all

of those results together before dividing. On the bottom of our division,

we take the independent variable and subtract the mean of the

independent variable, but then we square that result. Once we do this to

all of them, we add all the results together. Here it is in Python. I prefer

to view math in code quite often rather than the equation:

```
independent_var =
[2.5,8.5,5.5,4,7,10,1,4,5.5,5]
independent_mean = 5.3
```

```
dependent_var =
[5,17,11,8,14,20,2,8,11,10]
dependent_mean = 10.6
def slope(independent_var,
independent_mean, dependent_var,
dependent_mean):
    d = []
    x = []
    top = 0
    y = 0
    for i in
range(len(independent_var)):

        x.append(independent_var[i] -
independent_mean)
        for i in
range(len(dependent_var)):
            d.append(dependent_var[i]
- dependent_mean)
        for i in range(len(x)):
            top += x[i] * d[i]
        for i in
range(len(independent_var)):
            y += (independent_var[i]
- independent_mean)**2
        print(top/y)
        return top/y
pass
```

As you can see, it's relatively basic in what needs to be done but

you now need to feed it into the other side of the equation.

$$b_0 = \bar{y} - b_1\bar{x}$$

The answer to our slope was 2. This will now be multiplied

against the independent mean (x bar) and subtracted from the dependent

mean (y bar) to equal b_0. In our case, using the modified algorithm:

```
independent_var =
[2.5,8.5,5.5,4,7,10,1,4,5.5,5]
independent_mean = 5.3
dependent_var =
[5,17,11,8,14,20,2,8,11,10]
dependent_mean = 10.6
def slope(independent_var,
independent_mean, dependent_var,
dependent_mean):
    d = []
    x = []
    top = 0
    y = 0
    for i in
range(len(independent_var)):

        x.append(independent_var[i] -
independent_mean)
        for i in
range(len(dependent_var)):
            d.append(dependent_var[i]
- dependent_mean)
        for i in range(len(x)):
            top += x[i] * d[i]
        for i in
range(len(independent_var)):
```

```
            y += (independent_var[i] -
independent_mean)**2
        print(top/y)
        return top/y
pass
def y_intercept(independent_mean,
dependent_mean, slope):
        return (dependent_mean - (slope
* independent_mean))
        pass
print(y_intercept(independent_mean,de
pendent_mean,slope(independent_var,in
dependent_mean,dependent_var,dependen
t_mean)))
```

This means that the value is 0, which is not surprising in our

case but now we've got to put this back into slope intercept form. Here,

that would be:

$$\hat{y}_i = 0 + 2x$$

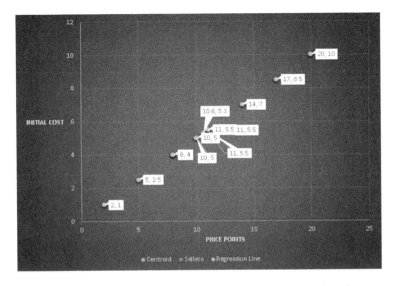

As you can see from this graph, the Regression Line is a completely perfect match, which means we have done the right calculations.

Why use Regression Analysis?

There Are Two Primary Reasons: Reason 1 Correlation and Importance

Regression analysis allows us to see if two variables have a correlation with each other if we decide to study those two variables. For instance, let's say that the variable that we used to determine our price points was based off of how much it cost the seller to buy it from the manufacturer. If the seller or sellers rather had a consistent method of charging a certain amount of money above others, it will show clearly within our graph. Remember that regression analysis is really the study of two different variables to see if that those variables have a correlation. Therefore, the variable that determines the price point of the seller will rise equally for the amount of money the seller bought the material or trinket from the manufacturer. The beautiful part about regression analysis is that once we put it into a graph, it becomes conceptually clear to us that there is a correlation by drawing a statistically significant line that represents the rate of change. If one can draw a line almost perfectly through the two data points and there is no sum of squared errors, then there is a high likelihood that there is a correlation between the two variables.

When we are dealing with massive amounts of information, we have to find a way to determine what information is important and what information is just a waste of our time. Let us say that we have a spreadsheet that tells us the day the trinket was sold on, the hour that the trinket was sold in, the city the trinket was sold in, the name of the person who sold the trinket, the street that trinket was bought on, the building number that the street that the trinket was bought on was in relation to, and the locations of where the materials for the trinket was sourced from. This spreadsheet is an absolute nightmare in terms of how much data you have to sit through because what if you have over a thousand different sellers on this list and there doesn't seem to be any correlation between them?

Regression analysis allows you to take each category and compare it to each other. In the list of items that are in our data sheet, we would have 7 different sets of data we would need to compare. Of those seven, it is most likely that we could create an association between where it was sold and where it was made. These would be negligible findings, but they would still have an association. With regression analysis, we are able to determine whether it is an important variable that we need to research. For instance, yes, it is likely that all of the trinkets were made in the same location. This doesn't really have a great importance other than knowing where it came from. Likewise, there's also, probably, not much significance to the name of the person who sold it since we are buying it from several different sellers, the building number that's near the place you bought it from, and a few others. What's more important is likely to be in association with the day that it was sold on, the street that the trinket was sold on, and maybe where the materials were sourced from. The reason why I say that these might be important is because we know that there are certain days of the week where items are on sale versus items that are sold at their normal price. We know that it is more likely that a seller will place a deal on an item that doesn't sell very well on their slowest day of the week. We also know that if the resources are more expensive to source from that this will ultimately lead to a higher price. These have reasons behind them that can be further explored, whereas the other ones don't have a direct correlation and thus don't have a direct importance to the exploratory search that is regression analysis.

Reason 2: Supervised Learning

The other reason to use regression analysis is because regression analysis is how you perform supervised learning. When you are testing the variables inside of a neural network, you are performing a regression analysis at every layer of your network. Let us look at how we might Define a line in a picture. Theoretically, you could Define a line as saying that in order for it to be a vertical line you must have a significant contrast difference between the previous pixel value, the current pixel value, and the next pixel value. You could create a matrix that looks like this:

$$\begin{bmatrix} 000 \\ 010 \\ 010 \\ 010 \end{bmatrix}$$

This is the beginning of a pattern recognition program, another form of a neural network. In this neural network you are comparing two values at a time. You compare the previous pixel value with the current pixel value and then you compare the current pixel value with the next pixel value. This ultimately determines whether there is a significant importance to the pixel you are currently on and this is how pattern recognition programs work, except that they have different equations and different matrices to handle different patterns. When you have to compare two variables at a time, you will be utilizing linear regression or regression analysis. I say linear regression or regression analysis because there is more than one type of regression analysis, linear regression is just the most common. Linear regression refers to the fact that you can plot a linear line between the differences.

Clustering Analysis using Python

What is Clustering Analysis?

There is no one-way of doing a cluster analysis and it is more of a concept than a specific type of algorithm. I suppose the best way to describe the difference is to utilize two examples. Let's say that our first example is that of cat and dogs. How might you go about classifying these two animals? Well, you know that you'll generally look for differences. Now, be careful because **cluster analysis is abstractly defined**. This means that you cannot check for specific features, you are just looking for things that are true of all living things. Therefore, you might look for size, width, and other physical features. Let's say you created a cluster analysis that could tell the difference between cats and dogs.

Now, could you see the same success if you applied this algorithm to trying to cluster server motherboards and personal computer motherboards? Honestly, the most you would get is an almost fair success rate of size. This is because motherboards like the

Raspberry Pi can actually be a server motherboard. You would have to develop a different algorithm based on different **abstract** parameters. Cluster Analysis requires that you not know ahead of time what features you are specifically looking for. You have to rely on trying to find any differences at all without knowing which difference will make the most impact because you don't know what features your area of interest will have.

How is Clustering Analysis different from previous Machine Learning algorithms?

Previously, Machine Learning algorithms had a primal understanding of what it needed to sift through. For cats and dogs, it knew that it would need to pay attention to the facial features as well as the shape of the animal itself. These features would be fine-tuned so that it would be much easier to pick up those features. The key aspect of these features is that they have finite parameters built on abstract concepts. Cluster Analysis allows a machine learning algorithm to have abstract parameters on abstract concepts.

Therefore, let's say that we're trying to find things that are worth looking into about a population. Instead of finding things to search for ourselves, we simply input what we know about a population and feed it to a cluster algorithm that attempts to sort and cluster relative data. The data that does cluster are the success zones of our algorithm and they become the new topic for further exploratory analysis.

A Theoretical Analysis of Clustering Analysis

Perhaps the most popular means of performing a Cluster Analysis is with the K means algorithm. Clustering, itself, is usually a part of the Discrete Unsupervised Learning algorithms group. This is how the K means Clustering algorithm works:

1. You make a best guess of how many K centroids you will need to make.

2. You systematically organize those K centroids to better align themselves with the clusters they are nearby finding the Euclidean distance.

3. Those new K centroids are now your labels for your clustered
    data.

So, since you basically know what a centroid is, we need
to cover what Euclidean distance is, which is *this* calculation:

$$\sqrt{\sum_{i=1}^{n}(a_i - p_i)^2}$$

You might think that this equation looks blindingly complex,
but it is important to note that this is simply calculating the Straight-
Line distance between 2 points. To break it down into a more simplistic
and less abrasive equation, this is what it looks like for 2 dimensions:

$$d = \sqrt{(x_2 - x_1)^2 + (y_2 - y_1)^2}$$

Or, alternatively,

$$d = \sqrt{(x_1 - x_2)^2 + (y_1 - y_2)^2}$$

As you can see, this form of the equation is far less scary and so
long as you have 2 sets of coordinates, you can just plug in the numbers

to get your result. The previous equation is for the Nth dimension, which means it calculates for more than 1 set and it is iterative. Literally, it translates to "calculate the sum of each of the indices, starting with one, as the subtraction of pair 1 index 1 and pair 2 index 1, squared and each consecutive pair. Then square root the entirety of the sum". Here is a Python implementation of the Euclidean distance:

```
import math
a_array = [(10, 1),(9,
6),(3,2),(7,4),(8,5)]
p_array =
[(8,3),(7,4),(5,9),(2,10),(6,1)]
def euclidean_distance(a_array, p_array):
    result = 0
    for i in range(len(a_array)):
        x_1 = a_array[i][0]
        x_2 = p_array[i][0]
        y_1 = a_array[i][1]
        y_2 = p_array[i][1]
        result += (x_1 - x_2)**2 +
(y_1 - y_2)**2
    return math.sqrt(result)
print(euclidean_distance(a_array,p_array)
)
```

Working Clustering Analysis in a Real-World Application with Results

Alright, so for this (and for licensing reasons) I have generated a random spreadsheet with data. There are 1,000 companies with their injury percentages, employee counts, and the percentages of whether they have safety goggles and gloves or not. The goal of this cluster analysis is to determine whether there is any relationship between these numbers. Let's look at the Employee Count vs Injuries:

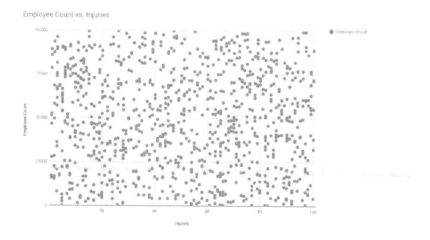

As we can see, it definitely doesn't look like it's associated based on raw numbers. If we look at Goggles and Gloves, we'll see the same thing.

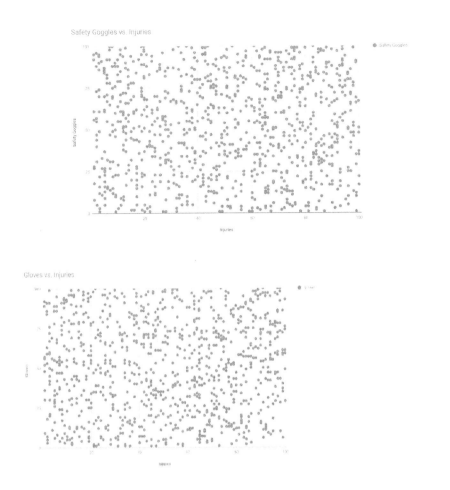

So, since we don't find an easy correlation there, let's abstract the Percentage of Injuries vs Employee Count by studying the number of Employees injured vs Employees.

Employees Injured vs. Employee Count

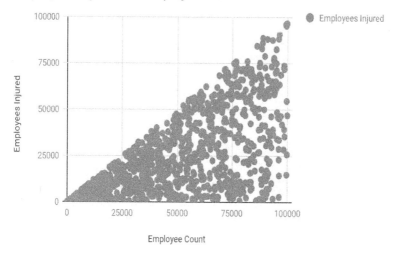

Wow! That's one heck of a difference that made. At this very moment we've successfully performed a cluster analysis, without having to do complicated math, and can determine that for this data there is a strong correlation between how many employees one has and how many injuries they have. Remember that Cluster Analysis does not have one right way of doing it, so even if you are able to clearly tell from this graph and did not have to use an algorithm like K-means to get there, it still represents Cluster Analysis. However, in a normal practice, we would then try to see if there was an underlying association for this, but for this example and brevity, I believe this is sufficient.

Implementing an Artificial Neural Network

What are Artificial Neural Networks?

Artificial neural networks are a classification of algorithm mixed with conceptual analysis of how biology, psychology, and circuitry integration work.

What is Conceptual Analysis?

A lot of people equate conceptual analysis to being that of philosophizing about a concept. The problem is that philosophizing about a specific topic, while useful in its own right, doesn't really break down the aspects of how to associate such concepts of philosophy to real-world Applications. Philosophy is the art of getting to the root of something via a route of logical reasoning. This is in fact a very useful tool in the programming world, the problem is that it's not conceptual analysis.

The best way to describe conceptual analysis is if you were to take a beer opener that you bought at a local convenience store and used it to open a soda bottle, the old ones. In such a case, you have made an association between the old type of soda bottle and the current type of glass beer. The beer opener works for both of them, but as the name denotes it was specifically designed for only opening beer. What we have done here is we have made a conceptual analysis of the device and found a different use for it. We understand the beer opener as a device that lifts metal lids off of glass containers if that lid meets a certain shape. Therefore, while only intended for opening beer bottles, we have analyzed the soda bottle and found that we can use the beer opener to open that type of bottle. The definition is to take a concept, look at it carefully, and see if that concept can be applied elsewhere.

The Study of Biology

The concept of the computer and, in fact, neural networks actually comes from our days of biology. There are three levels of Sciences, which each science ultimately led to the next science. However, biology was the start of it all. Biology is the study of life and how life works. When scientists began studying the physical makeup of the brain, they eventually came to find out that the brain was capable of housing electricity. However, the concept of a computer was envisioned even before that. All you need to do in order to effectively envision a computer is to think of something that causes a chain reaction. Perhaps my favorite study of computer mechanisms has to deal with enormous Domino puzzles where they use the Domino's to ultimately calculate a binary equation.

The term computer was actually invented around the 1600s where a writer referred to an accountant or person who worked with numbers all day as a computer or a person who computes calculations. We have had computers for a long time if computers are, indeed, this definition. As humans, we have tried to take the repetitive mechanisms of our daily life out of our lives. The first repetitive mechanism we tried to remove was the necessity to do mathematics with nothing more than a pen and paper. Perhaps my favorite example of this is the famous abacus. We do this by studying our own lives and then inventing a machine or mechanism that can ultimately do those repetitive tasks. The more we increased our mathematical knowledge, which is what was required in order to build these machines, the more the concept of a computer came into existence.

The Study of Circuitry

The study of mathematics and biology, along with the constant need to make our daily lives better, eventually led to the creation of circuitry. Thomas Edison is often credited as the first individual to ever create a successful light bulb while Isaac Newton is famous for a Litany of mathematical achievements, for which one of those came the concept of Wi-Fi. However, electricity itself was a subject that was of great interest to many of the ancient civilizations. In fact, it's rumored that some Mediterranean cultures had a sort of magic that allowed them to rub material on cat fur that would attract bird feathers. We have had laws of magnetism for centuries now, but the study of electricity ultimately came from studying how objects in life interact with each other.

However, it wasn't until around 1791 to about the middle 1800s that we truly began investing electricity into our lives. It was in this area of time that the famous Volta battery and Faraday Motor was invented, which was also during the time that the study of electromagnetism became a real thing. Once we hit the 19th century, scientists were basically coming out of the woodwork on electrical theories, concepts, and inventions. These different scientists would eventually become the linchpin of how electricity works and then it was only a matter of time until we reached computers.

The Study of Psychology

Now, up until this point, I haven't really mentioned anything about neural networks according to the Sciences. However, it's around the psychology and conceptual analysis of the human mind that neural networks truly began to emerge. The purpose of psychology is the study of the psyche or the mind in most of our definitions. This meant that there was an entire science solely dedicated to figuring out how we figure things out. Because of our understanding of biology, we understood that there had to be a chain of events that led to where we were. Because of our understanding of circuitry, we understood that the mechanism for delivering information inside of our bodies was usually done with electricity.

These two concepts had a profound impact when we started studying how the mind makes decisions. While the neuron of a human mind is somewhat more sophisticated, it was understood that every question only ever had two answers. In fact, you can think of complicated questions that have more than one answer as a question tree. The human neuron takes electricity inside and then makes a choice as to whether the electricity will leave its neuron to go down another path or if it just stays there. Therefore, the question will result in an activation or a no activation. Yes, every question really has only two answers. The understanding of this concept meant that if you could create a decision algorithm, that could run in parallel with other algorithms like this, and the algorithm had a choice to activate or not activate then you could conceptually create a human neuron. That is, ultimately, the idea of a neural network but because computers are not humans, there are some complications.

Backpropagation - Linchpin of The Neural Network

This leads us to backpropagation, which is the linchpin of neural networking in general. Backpropagation is really just a mathematical optimization, which is, essentially, what all of neural networking really is. It takes a mathematical solution and optimizes for a better result, which is probably why so many people find it confusing.

Let us start off by examining what our neural network is made up of:

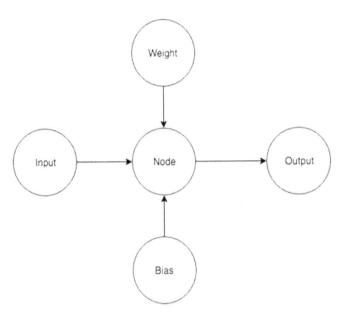

As you can see, there aren't many variables to take into account. In fact, it can really be summed up quite sequentially:

$$O = w + b + i$$

This makes for a rather simplistic looking equation, but now we need to add some complexity. Since we know that neural networks are made up of several nodes and not just one, let's go ahead and say we have 2 nodes. Well, now the equation has a cost to it. The reason why it has a cost to it is because Node 1 has to reach a certain value to send a value to Node 2 and Node 2 now has to combine its' value with Node 1 to reach a certain value to send its' value to Output. We will denote each Node as a and then each layer as a superscript L with a subtraction of 1 for each layer it is away from the output. Thus, our equation is now:

$$O = C = a^L + a^{L-n}$$

Therefore, the output is really the cost which is the combination of the last layer and all other layers a depends on (linearly so far) represented as n. Therefore, on the reverse side of this, we could actually say that our equation is this:

$$C(...) = (a^L - O)^2$$

Now, you might argue that this is a different equation and it definitely is because the output is now subtracted from what will ultimately be the value coming from the last layer. This is when you have a **desired** output and *not* when you just assign your output as the cost. Additionally, we have to make a change to our previous equation. Since we have more than one layer, we now have to add this in.

$$a^L = \sigma(w^L a^{L-1} + b^L)$$

So, let's breakdown what this is doing. Our very first node is

a^{L-1}, which now affects the outcome of a^L. The value from that

previous node is now multiplied against the weight value of our current

node. Then we add the bias in before utilizing our **Activation Function**

or, in this case, the sigmoid calculation. The Activation function

ultimately determines if the value is significant enough to send a signal

to the next node. At this point we have reached the calculation needed

for a **Feedforward Network** or otherwise called a Neural Network by

most. Feedforward means the information is being fed forward by the

math.

Now we're gonna get into some Calculus because we have to

talk about Derivatives. Essentially, we're trying to find out how much

each variable the ultimate cost is *derived* from. So, here's a dump of

math:

$$\frac{\partial C_0}{\partial w^L} = \frac{\partial x^L}{\partial w^L} \frac{\partial a^L}{\partial x^L} \frac{\partial C_0}{\partial a^L}$$

I know, I know. It's a lot to stuff down, so let's take small bites. What this is saying is that a variation in the Cost over a variation in the weight is equivalent to the variation in the previous layer output (denoted by x) over the current variation of weight, multiplied by the variation of the current layer value over the previous layer value variation, and finally multiplied by the current variant cost over the current layer value. I know, still a lot to take in but you can think of each one being based off of each other. You effect one set of ratios and all of the rest change with it and you change those ratios by either messing with the weights or biases, but this utilizes the weights ratio. To calculate for the biases, you simply switch the positioned weights with the values of the bias. This is known as the **Chain rule**. There is a bit more math to have a multi-layer multi-node network, but essentially you just now have to add indices to keep track of those values and add in the additional sums that come from multi-connected nodes. The understanding of these values and the manipulation of these values is *how* backpropagation works, which you then add these to the gradient descent concept I presented earlier. The reason why I am avoiding going all out is because, we would need to mathematically map

something equivalent to this:

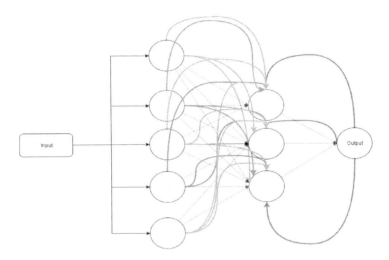

Take the principles you've just learned and add them to each

colored line you see in this photograph, so you can see why

understanding it is far more useful than walking through it. It's a very

large concept and it will take you quite some time to fully digest it.

Backpropagating - An Applicable Program

So, for this, I'm going to bring in some fellow programming

code as a real world applicable program for Backpropagation. The

following code is underneath the https://opensource.org/licenses/MIT

license and it is thanks to David Adler that we have this code. It was

published May 30 of 2012 at ActiveState. It is open source code.

```python
import math
import random
import string

class NN:
  def __init__(self, NI, NH, NO):
    # number of nodes in layers
    self.ni = NI + 1 # +1 for bias
    self.nh = NH
    self.no = NO

    # initialize node-activations
    self.ai, self.ah, self.ao = [],[], []
    self.ai = [1.0]*self.ni
    self.ah = [1.0]*self.nh
    self.ao = [1.0]*self.no

    # create node weight matrices
    self.wi = makeMatrix (self.ni,
self.nh)
    self.wo = makeMatrix (self.nh,
self.no)
    # initialize node weights to random
vals
    randomizeMatrix ( self.wi, -0.2, 0.2 )
    randomizeMatrix ( self.wo, -2.0, 2.0 )
    # create last change in weights
matrices for momentum
    self.ci = makeMatrix (self.ni,
self.nh)
    self.co = makeMatrix (self.nh,
self.no)

  def runNN (self, inputs):
    if len(inputs) != self.ni-1:
      print 'incorrect number of inputs'
```

```
    for i in range(self.ni-1):
      self.ai[i] = inputs[i]

    for j in range(self.nh):
      sum = 0.0
      for i in range(self.ni):
        sum +=( self.ai[i] * self.wi[i][j]
)
      self.ah[j] = sigmoid (sum)

    for k in range(self.no):
      sum = 0.0
      for j in range(self.nh):
        sum +=( self.ah[j] * self.wo[j][k]
)
      self.ao[k] = sigmoid (sum)

    return self.ao



  def backPropagate (self, targets, N, M):
      #
http://www.youtube.com/watch?v=aVId8KMsdUU
&feature=BFa&list=LL1dMCkmXl4j9_v0HeKdNcRA

    # calc output deltas
    # we want to find the instantaneous
rate of change of ( error with respect to
weight from node j to node k)
    # output_delta is defined as an
attribute of each ouput node. It is not
the final rate we need.
    # To get the final rate we must
multiply the delta by the activation of
```

```
    the hidden layer node in question.
    # This multiplication is done
according to the chain rule as we are
taking the derivative of the activation
function
    # of the ouput node.
    # dE/dw[j][k] = (t[k] - ao[k]) * s'(
SUM( w[j][k]*ah[j] ) ) * ah[j]
    output_deltas = [0.0] * self.no
    for k in range(self.no):
      error = targets[k] - self.ao[k]
      output_deltas[k] =  error *
dsigmoid(self.ao[k])

    # update output weights
    for j in range(self.nh):
      for k in range(self.no):
        # output_deltas[k] * self.ah[j] is
the full derivative of
dError/dweight[j][k]
        change = output_deltas[k] *
self.ah[j]
        self.wo[j][k] += N*change +
M*self.co[j][k]
        self.co[j][k] = change

    # calc hidden deltas
    hidden_deltas = [0.0] * self.nh
    for j in range(self.nh):
      error = 0.0
      for k in range(self.no):
        error += output_deltas[k] *
self.wo[j][k]
      hidden_deltas[j] = error *
dsigmoid(self.ah[j])
```

```
        #update input weights
        for i in range (self.ni):
          for j in range (self.nh):
            change = hidden_deltas[j] *
self.ai[i]
            #print
'activation',self.ai[i],'synapse',i,j,'cha
nge',change
            self.wi[i][j] += N*change +
M*self.ci[i][j]
            self.ci[i][j] = change

        # calc combined error
        # 1/2 for differential convenience &
**2 for modulus
        error = 0.0
        for k in range(len(targets)):
          error = 0.5 * (targets[k]-
self.ao[k])**2
        return error


    def weights(self):
      print 'Input weights:'
      for i in range(self.ni):
        print self.wi[i]
      print
      print 'Output weights:'
      for j in range(self.nh):
        print self.wo[j]
      print ''

    def test(self, patterns):
      for p in patterns:
        inputs = p[0]
        print 'Inputs:', p[0], '-->',
```

```python
        self.runNN(inputs), '\tTarget', p[1]

    def train (self, patterns,
max_iterations = 1000, N=0.5, M=0.1):
        for i in range(max_iterations):
            for p in patterns:
                inputs = p[0]
                targets = p[1]
                self.runNN(inputs)
                error =
self.backPropagate(targets, N, M)
            if i % 50 == 0:
                print 'Combined error', error
        self.test(patterns)


def sigmoid (x):
    return math.tanh(x)

# the derivative of the sigmoid function
in terms of output
# proof here:
#
http://www.math10.com/en/algebra/hyperboli
c-functions/hyperbolic-functions.html
def dsigmoid (y):
    return 1 - y**2

def makeMatrix ( I, J, fill=0.0):
    m = []
    for i in range(I):
        m.append([fill]*J)
    return m

def randomizeMatrix ( matrix, a, b):
    for i in range ( len (matrix) ):
```

```
        for j in range ( len (matrix[0]) ):
            matrix[i][j] = random.uniform(a,b)

def main ():
    pat = [
        [[0,0], [1]],
        [[0,1], [1]],
        [[1,0], [1]],
        [[1,1], [0]]
    ]
    myNN = NN ( 2, 2, 1)
    myNN.train(pat)
if __name__ == "__main__":
    main()
```

How This Script and Others Like it Can be Useful

If you carefully look at the code, this book has a lot of what this code talks about, more than just backpropagation. The constructor class NN is actually making a Neural Node and several of them can make a neural network. It also has the functionality to run that network and then backpropagate. This script is useful because it is a generalize script that allows you to use it in multiple scenarios and can be modified for your needs. Honestly, if you can fully understand *how* this script is working then you can understand *how* most neural networking and backpropagating scripts work.

The only con that I have with this script is that it needs to be modified to run on a Graphics card. This is great if you're running it on a PC without much information, but in order to get a power network you need a lot of cores. They are now selling "AI" specific Graphics cards as a Neural Network can only handle as much work as much it has access to processing cores. However, understanding this script with propel you quickly through your work on Machine Learning.

A 90 Day Plan for Machine Learning with Python

Concept

Day 0 - Day 7

The first seven days of this project should be dedicated to thinking about what you really want from your neural network. You should not spend these seven days just lounging about, but, rather, you should spend this time to discuss it with friends of the same mental capacity or colleagues to go over it as a concept. You should almost never make a blank statement of "I want to create [this] because of [this]" as it almost never works. This should really be a time where you take the time to refine the concept.

During the conversation, you should cover a few bases to ensure that this program is built and is built with the best purpose and moral intentions. When you build a neural network, you should question its' purpose. It might be fantastic to build a neural network that identifies the type of fecal matter something is, but what use does it have and where can you apply it? If it has a use, can you further refine that use so that it is specialized? Specializing reduces the amount of work that needs to be done in order to get a working product. The further you can specialize a neural network, the further that you can modulate this network. Modulation means networks can be developed in parallel, which means they can take a shorter amount of time to get done if the neural network is developed by a team.

Not only do you need to find out the specialization capabilities and what you can modulate, but you also need to know where to apply it and how to apply it. Let us take the algorithm that Google got in trouble with a few years back for as an example.

To put it as I understood what happened, Google created an algorithm that would determine the most associated searches towards a phrase. It was later found that if you made a search referencing a white man, job and work-related references were likely to show up. However, if you made the same search referencing a colored individual, you were more likely to see services where one could take a look at jail-time records and offenses. The reason why it ended up like this was because the network had found a correlation of women doing biased background checks on colored men versus white men. While there is a political stance here, there was a populated uproar against this result and the talk of racial bias in programming began. Therefore, when you go about creating a program that's allowed to "learn", you really need to also conceptualize where the program can go wrong.

During these discussions, you should really be recording them so that you can review them after this period.

Definition and Flow Charts

Day 8 - Day 14

Once you have spent quite some time on the concept, it's time to finally lay it down on paper. Provided you recorded the conversations you had, this step should be rather simplistic in nature. It's really important to define how the neural network is going to work and while you may have conceptualized and plugged up any holes during the concept phase, during the flowchart phase is when you begin to find how your particular neural network is going to operate. It's during this time that you really need to think about where the potential outliers that you don't want into the system will bake itself into the system.

Additionally, it is during this time that you can begin to conceptualize how long the neural network is going to take. Just to let you know, the more neural nodes that you can run, the less time it's going to take to ultimately train that Network. This means that you have to break the concepts down into their very, most basic elements in order for it to work at a fast and efficient rate. Flowcharts also help you determine which layers you're going to develop and in what order. Usually, most beginning networks start off with 1 to 2 hidden layers with an input and an output layer.

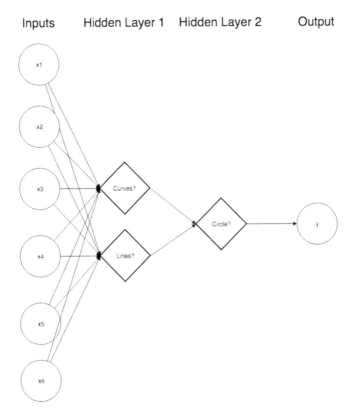

Hidden Layer 1 Development

Day 15 - Day 21

The hidden layer is where all of your neurons will ultimately be working, and it is named The Hidden Layer because you and your team are likely the only ones who will ever see it. A lot of people who use the hidden area will ultimately only ever see the inputs that they are using and seeing the result of the area that's hidden. It is during this time that you really need to try to get the most rudimentary algorithms down. During this phase, you should not be concerning yourself with optimization or trying to correct the algorithm itself. Instead, you should be developing a very basic notion of how the algorithm is to work and then putting that into practice.

A lot of time is wasted in neural networks by trying to optimize your first go at a neural network or a specific type of neural network. There are a lot of ways to optimize algorithms so that they move faster, but that's not your goal in this first step. This first step should really be about trying to lay down the foundation of the beginnings of the first area of your neural network. Once you're able to test it and see that it works in a way that you kind of want it to work, then you can begin to make optimizations to make it faster and this is actually where correcting your neural network comes in.

Supervised Learning and Corrections

Day 22 - Day 28

During this particular set of days, you should be paying   . attention to the different weights and biases that your neural network is employing. It is also during this time that if you begin to see successful results, you now need to pay attention to how fast you are getting those results. Depending on the speed of the results, if you have any neural networks designed to rely on how fast a reaction happens, the speed of your algorithms could change the effect that the neural network has. Therefore, once you begin seeing that your neural network is working with a training set and doing very well, it's time to optimize the algorithms you're using.

The reason why I mention optimizing algorithms is because while doing individual tests may only take somewhere around a minute to two minutes, you have to expand that amount by the number of people going to be affected by this neural network. Therefore, if you have a billion people utilizing this neural network then you have to take into account that if it takes a minute or two to test this neural network then it is going to take a billion times a minute or two in order to test it on that scale. Once you have made some modifications to your algorithms so that they're faster and you are getting better results, it's now time to head into the next phase.

Unsupervised Learning and Corrections

Day 29 - Day 35

Now it's time to let your algorithm just run wild at this point and see what happens with it. There isn't really a way about going and doing a randomized test, but what most people do is they take enormous amounts of data from a company that may give it away freely or may sell it at a price and then do their tests on that data. The difference between supervised learning and unsupervised learning is that supervised learning is where you know what the answers will be for the output should your algorithm be designed correctly. Unsupervised learning is where you have no idea whether or not the output is correct without doing a manual calculation yourself as to what should happen. In fact, unsupervised learning is often utilized to find the necessary labels you might need for supervised learning.

Now, this is not to say that unsupervised learning is appropriate for all learning algorithms or neural networks. In fact, there are some cases where it makes sense to not do any unsupervised learning because you can always generate labels for the input that's coming into the neural network. In this case, you would simply just further optimize and test your neural network in much bigger batches. The idea of unsupervised learning is so that your algorithm is capable of defining its own labels for the inputs that it sees. The reason why there are so many neural networks out there is because there are just so many situations in which you might need one network over another. It really depends on what you're doing with your neural network.

Hidden Layer 2 Development

Day 36 - Day 42

Now it's time to take your current one hidden area network and expanded into further complexity. When you developed the flowchart, you should have gone from the most complex topics to the most basic topics to where one of two items would be the answer for the question. Now it is time to go up in complexity so that your neural network can become fully developed. Depending on the actual topic you chose to create a neural network, you may need more than two hidden layers in order to actually do all of the necessary calculations. However, this would also expand this much further than 90 days and most people don't really need to utilize more than two layers.

The reason why most people don't need more than two layers is because what they are usually trying to do is a two-step process. You can often determine how many layers you're going to need by how many steps it takes to get to the output that you want. However, even if you do have more than one layer you tend to want to lower the number of layers that you might have because of the potential problem of the infinite gradient. The more layers that you have in a network, the more likely you're going to run up against the infinite gradient. Therefore, you should really spend about a week developing each additional layer and then spending about 2 weeks testing each layer so that they are compatible.

Supervised Learning and Corrections
Day 43 - Day 49

This time is going to be a little bit different than the last time that you tested your network because not only are you testing the first layer of your network but you're also testing the second layer of your network. It is important to realize this because your second layer is going to be based off of both how you created that layer but also how successful the previous layer is. This is why you need to ultimately keep track of the outputs of the first layer before they go into the second layer so that you can catch on to problems before they become unmanageable.

Additionally, once you begin seeing success in this area you also need to see if there are unnecessary nodes. One of the problems when developing a neural network is that your original conceptualization and flowchart design may take into account unnecessary elements. For instance, if I am trying to detect whether an object is a nose or not then I would likely want to detect whether there are holes such as a circle and whether there is a general shape of a nose. Instead of detecting for curvatures, which is detecting circles, I would really just need to text whether there are two Shadows that are parallel. Detecting whether a pixel is darker than the previous pixel is far easier then detecting whether something curves. In such a case, it would actually be a optimization to change it to the simpler equation.

Unsupervised Learning and Corrections

Day 50 - Day 56

During this next phase, you should both be preparing to handle unknown data but also be exploring potential ways to reduce your neural network when possible. After this phase, you are likely to go through an Alpha Testing session where you unleash this neural network amongst the wild. Up until this point, almost all of the data that you have had needs to be static data. What I mean by Static data is even though you don't know what the data may result in, ultimately you know that there's only a specific amount of data that's going to be tested. When I refer to Dynamic data, I am referring to data that will either change while in use or data that has no seeming end to it. One of the problems that neural networking has to deal with is the sheer size of the tasks that are required to completely handle the problem the neural network was designed to handle. You can think of Google's voice typing as an example of such a situation. While they probably tested it on known datasets, the neural network now has to contend with an almost never-ending stream of data. Therefore, not only should you be determining whether your algorithm is working correctly but you should also be exploring the best avenues for deployment.

Now, you may have an economic prediction algorithm that is designed to try and figure out where the statistics of the stock market is going. Even in such a case where you would essentially only be running the machine on your computer, you also have to consider just how many businesses are on the stock market. Your test sample sizes might have only been utilizing 10 to 20 companies at a time because you only have one server core. This is the true test of optimization and a location of study for neural networks. You will likely need to create some sort of server Farm unless you are able to reduce the amount of calculations down to something that could be handled by a single server, but you are likely going to need at least a few graphics cards because each calculation has to be done by a core.

Alpha Testing

Day 57 - Day 63

Alpha Testing is a closed group testing and it really depends on what type of neural network you are developing as to whether you will essentially need Alpha Testing or not. Rather, it depends on what type of neural network you are developing that will determine whether you need people to be involved or if you can simply just let your algorithm into the wild.

The best way that I can describe Alpha Testing for new programmers is imagine if you were to make the most basic version of a product. You know that it's going to take at least half a year for you to make the full product that you want to make but you have no idea whether your idea for a product is going to be good or not. The truth of the matter is that the only way that you can check whether a product is going to be good or not is if you test it.

Let's discuss how big companies go about Alpha Testing their products because you and I are unknowingly apart of this. When Apple decided to begin developing facial recognition on their mobile devices, it became very apparent that Apple might have not done it in the most morally correct way that they could have. They claimed to have tested the technology against millions of faces but how did they get those millions of faces?

What most people don't know is that this facial recognition software is not a machine learning algorithm in the normal sense. Instead, what you have is a neural network that was developed to do one task really well that stays on the phone. This means that this neural network only gets upgrades when the entire phone actually does an upgrade. Unlike a normal neural network, which receives updates regularly over the internet, this is a neural network that works in a type of stasis where it has one specific track that stays common no matter what phone it is on. However, the implicit agreement occurred when you decided to buy a new phone. In order to get this new technology, you actually had to go buy a brand-new phone that was considered the flagship phone of that time. You became a Beta tester in this case and we have seen the results of this new technology. The Alpha Test was done within the company, a company that isn't heavy in diversity when it comes to their work staff. Therefore, you also heard issues with Americans that had a melatonin range not within Caucasian limits, which Apple blamed on deadlines. Alpha testing can propel or hinder your efforts depending on how you carry it out.

Feedback Reception and Corrections

Day 64 - Day 70

During this period, you should begin learning about the success rates of your neural network depending on how you Alpha tested it. It is during this time that you are either extending the amount of time you need to develop the neural that work, essentially going back to scratch and figuring out why your feedback was so negative, or you begin to head down the route of finding out how you're going to do Beta Testing. During an alpha test, your testers should be relatively close and there should generally be a non-disclosure agreement between who you're testing with. This is because you should only have a small population of people you should be testing at this point in time so that you can get a general idea of how successful it is on a much grander scale.

Additionally, this is the time that you need to make several different types of statistical analysis about how your neural network is working with unknown elements. This is because neural networks are never finished, and I don't really understand how companies can't seem to understand this. When you develop a neural network, you are developing a system that is always going to need change in order to become more accurate. You can't simply develop a neural network and just leave it be because it's as accurate as it is ever going to be. In fact, almost no website works like this. It is there in this stage that you begin to figure out how you're going to improve and expand on your neural network as a basic concept because once you develop a neural network, you have to begin finding out ways you can further apply that neural network. Mind you, this is tackling the subject from a business point of view. If you are just developing a neural network for fun, it's really just about the statistical analysis that will tell you where the weak parts of your neural network are. It's important to go through this step even if you're not going to deploy this in a business environment because it makes you more familiar with the process of doing this in a production environment.

Beta Testing

Day 71 - Day 77

During this period of time you should now be beta testing the technology, which means that you need to find a public way of releasing it and incentivizing complete strangers to download and test your technology. Most big companies offer incentives such as payment for people who beta test their technology because usually the beta testers are put into some type of situation where they have to work on a regular basis. The best-case example that I can think about explaining this with is the Uber driving experiment where the drivers were supposed to be Uber drivers but, at the same time, they mostly allowed the car to drive itself. This is a fairly new concept of self-driving cars that has come onto the market but has received serious backlash because of how dangerous this could be. Therefore, Uber has to pay somebody to be in the car and pay attention to what the car is doing so that the car doesn't actually put anyone at risk for their life. There were a few incidences where the driver actually fell asleep or wasn't paying attention and the car made a miscalculation or a mistake, which wound up with the injury of another as a result of it.

As a person who may just be creating a neural network to run in the wild, the best-case scenario I can think of where you would be able to test your neural network is to actually just share it with other machine learning enthusiasts. In fact, this would be a better route to take because they are far better at being able to provide you with critical feedback in what they experienced with your neural network. Most companies don't normally have this type of luxury though because when they did the Alpha Testing, they had the machine learning experts already critically analyze what it was doing and how it was doing it. It's a different situation for a hobbyist to do something like machine learning than a company to do it because the company usually has deep enough pockets to step things up much faster than the hobbyist. That doesn't make it impossible for the hobbyist, it just makes the process a little bit slower.

Feedback Reception and Corrections

Day 78 - Day 84

During this time, you should begin receiving feedback whether it is expertly put together or if it's just that your neural network didn't work for them. Feedback is useful no matter what level of grammatical correctness it comes from. Having had to sift through thousands of different reviews to see and gauge the feeling that I get from the public, all feedback will generally migrate towards key points that you should be paying attention to. The problem for many machine-learning enthusiasts in the very beginning is that they think that all feedback will either be good or bad. The truth of the matter is that feedback is a bit varied in the way that it's displayed, but the details are in the overall emotions that the reviewers reveal.

Perhaps the best way to describe it is an old type of doll that was sold before the 19th century. Let me tell you, those things are creepy. In fact, a lot of people agree with me that many of those types of dolls are creepy but the fact that they're creepy doesn't help. What does help is that they will often list the reason why it is creepy, which in this case is usually the eyes of the doll itself is the part that's creepy.

In a neural network, you will often see a habitual pattern as to what the neural network got wrong. Let us talk about facial recognition in such a mannerism. If you tested the facial recognition patterns and the overall feedback was that it didn't work in some cases, if you were given the ability to have feedback mechanisms such as the data that was associated with the face that the algorithm got wrong, you could see that it might be that you didn't account for nose variations. There are a lot of different noses out there and if you had followed the suggestion of just detecting two Shadows underneath the nose, there are noses that are shadowless because they are designed in a more crooked manner. It's just an evolutionary trait that you didn't take account of. It is during this time where you have randomized feedback that you're able to recognize the weak spots of your neural network and account for them before you go into production.

Production

Day 85 - Day 90

Now you should have reached the production cycle and the production cycle is basically where you find out where you can sell your product. This is more of the business side than anything to do with the machine learning site because at this point you now have a product and you are now spending your time finding a way to put that product into the hands of your customers.

Conclusion

Understanding Machine Learning

Unlike common misconceptions, machine learning, while it is a lot about a two-way decision, it is not simply about a bunch of if else statements. This concept is a very basic and generalized form of understanding what machine learning really is. However, in order to understand what machine learning is, you actually have to understand the intent of the program itself. The definition of insanity is to do the same thing over and over while expecting different results each time that you do it. The conception that machine learning is nothing more than a bunch of if else statements is the statement that machine learning does the same thing over and over. In fact, machine learning changes with each iteration that the if else statements run so while it is a bunch of if else statements, it is not linear programming. Instead, it is referred to as recursive programming. It's recursive because once it gets a result that is correct, it feeds that result back into its random set so that it can further along the gradient descent that you are trying to achieve.

This means that the programmers who assume that it is just a bunch of if else statements are partially correct but don't understand the underlying implications of what machine learning is. This is why it is very difficult to explain high-level concepts in very basic terms. It is a bunch of if else statements but with a different purpose than your average program.

This leads us to the next problem and that is that machine learning often has a specific form of algorithm and application. You will not utilize the same type of machine learning for population prediction or economic prediction that you might use for text-based prediction. This is because the algorithm has to take up data that comes in different forms and in different varieties, but more importantly is that the output is of a different intention. With population prediction and economic prediction, you are trying to find commonalities in between the data so that you can make better predictions as to how many people will be in a society in the future, which companies might do best during what periods, and essentially trying to predict what no normal human being could predict. On the other hand, a text-based prediction utilizes known mannerisms and parts of speech in order to determine what the next word of a sentence might be. These are two very different types of predictions, but one common thread that you will find between the two is that one set of predictions is based off of unpredictable data while the other set of predictions is based off of a predictable set of data.

This means that whenever you're developing a neural network, it's not just how the neural network has developed but with what intention that neural network will be developed. This is because neural networks are not generalized and almost all of them have a very specific purpose in mind. Unlike the human mind, neural networks are not designed to have staggering capabilities of adaptation. In fact, staggering capabilities of adaptation is not a humanoid trait because we adapt very slowly. It is common knowledge that you cannot spend a week trying to learn programming and understand all that there is about programming along with the best practices that come with programming. It takes a very long time to understand what is needed from you and how to go about doing it. Neural networks work in a very similar way and they are more linear than humans.

The Staggering Support of Python

A lot of people associate the success of python with the excessive Academia programming in general. I will have to say Python does a great job in the academic world where it applies to numbers and mathematical equations that need to be tested out very quickly. However, schools and places of learning are generally not the Pinnacle of what I see in terms of machine learning and applications for machine learning. In fact, most of the Python code in the world usually has very little to do with any Academia at all. The problem with computer science in general is that it has this image that it is only capable of existing because people go to school for it and you need to learn how to do things from school because you can't learn it in real life. There are two sides to this vision. You have the old school mentality that computers are an academic achievement and resource. You have the much newer version mentality that computers are primarily a source where you go to learn pretty much anything that you want. The problem here is that there are more people in charge with the vision of the older school of mentality than there are of the newer mentality. Most of the people working in technology, in the highest regions of technology, usually did not have any science degree whatsoever because depending on how they came about with technology that degree might not have actually been a degree that existed.

Python is primarily popular because it's very easy to get a hold of, it's very forgiving in terms of the syntax that allows the programming to follow, and it's a rather old programming language compared to other programming languages in existence. Adding on top of this are the different communities that surround the language itself. As we mentioned, Blender is a graphics modeling system and since that covers everything from movies to video games to even commercials nowadays, that's a huge crowd. Then you have Eve online, which is a massive multiplayer video game that allows you to develop add-ons to the system that have to be in the same code that the system was developed in. Combine the modeling community of Eve online with the modeling community of the Sims 4 and you have a very large base of people who are interested in not just making things but also altering things. The difference between making something and altering something is that altering something in programming means that you have to test the code that's there repeatedly to figure out how the programmers programmed the code. The code is not all there at once and you have to reverse engineer how the programmers worked out how they were going to build the game. It's a very difficult, time-consuming process that many experts in the field do on a daily basis when it comes to Advanced military weapons systems and similar actions. That means that this entire Community is heavily reliant on analysis and Mathematics, which lead us into why Python is so popular amongst machine-learning enthusiasm.

Machine Language just takes advantage of what's already there.

A Set Track to Set Your Neural Network into the Wild

Concept

You should always begin your neural networks by determining exactly what concepts you want to tackle in your neural network. You can go out and make the best neural network you could ever make without actually knowing what it was intended for, but the problem is that in order to make the best neural network for a singular task is that you have to know what that single task is going to be. Einstein took part in developing one of the worst weapons in the world and it is one of the best forms of Destruction in the world, but they weren't necessarily focused on making it the most destructive thing in the world. In fact, many people of the Manhattan Project regret that they ever took part in the Manhattan Project because of how much destruction it caused. They didn't have a true intention on exactly what it was that they were creating but rather a general concept of trying to make a weapon that might change the war. Yes, they did make a weapon that changed the war, but it was also the scariest weapon we have ever made. This is the very value that I've tried to convey that you need to consider when you make a neural network because while you may make a neural network, you don't always know exactly what that neural network is going to be used for unless you discuss it as a concept.

Design

Once you a fully figured out what your neural network is going to be as a concept, then it is time to lay down the foundations so that you can figure out how you can arrive at that concept in a morally obligated way. Your algorithm is not going to be the best if it prefers Caucasian faces over Asian faces or your algorithms not going to be the best if it only takes account for the profits of companies rather than the deficit of companies, which is actually where profit can be made. Additionally, this is where you begin laying out the infrastructure of how much you're going to need in order to get to the concept that you're trying to talk about or you're trying to design for. A lot of the problem with developing neural networks is finding out just how much resources you're going to need to make it work. Luckily, there are some Geniuses in the world that found very clever ways of developing a method of reducing the overall cost, but you still need to pay attention to how fast things are, how they will aggregate in much bigger quantities, and just how accurate your algorithms will be. This is not exactly the stage that you want to utilize to optimize these algorithms but rather make sure that your algorithm works in the first place and that you are able to scale that algorithm.

Develop

The development and testing phase are really one and the same, it's just that one happens before the other. In order to develop an algorithm, you have to do exploratory tests to find out what you're doing and then in order to improve upon an algorithm, you have to do tests. Therefore, in order to develop algorithms further you have to test further and so these two really go hand-in-hand. The difference being is that during the development phase you are either creating algorithms or you are optimizing out for them, which can often stand for correcting. You ideally want to be handling both at the same time and creating enough checkpoints so that you can see where you, yourself, made a diverging change in the algorithm that might have led to what's known as a domino consequence. You have immediate errors that are easily recognizable and usually changeable on the spot. Then you have what's known as a domino error, and the only way that you are able to find out what your domino error is if you are able to keep track of where you change things.

Test

There's a difference between a closed testing environment, an initial testing environment, and a beta testing environment. During the initial testing environment, your concern should primarily be whether you're getting the correct outputs, whether your algorithms are working at a decent rate, and whether you have any areas that you can improve upon. The way that you can test whether your algorithms are working at a decent rate is both linear and parallel as well as serial. Linear testing simply means that each and every algorithm fits a Big O notation equation that is satisfactory. Big O notation simply refers to how fast an algorithm will work over a given amount of time. Parallel equation vs. serial equation is very different. In a parallel equation, you essentially want all the results to come out at about the same amount of time. In a parallel equation you have to deal with the slowest Link in that equation. This will determine how fast each layer in the network is going to go because your layer is only as fast as your slowest node. Serial equation simply refers to how fast a specific track of equations is able to calculate a result. Essentially, the serial equation will determine how fast you are able to go from one node to the next node to the output.

The best way that I could create a world example for this is a building of factory workers. Each level of factory workers can only hold so many Factory workers at a given time but each level that you add to it allows you to produce more products. Therefore, you have to find the rate at which the amount of factory workers and the amount of levels that you have produce a result that is successful at generating product at decent times. Therefore, linear testing is ensuring each worker is capable of working as fast you need them to. Parallel testing is ensuring how fast each floor of workers can produce results together. Finally, serial testing is how fast those results can be pushed out of the building as a final result.

Closed Testing

Closed testing is where your first bit of Randomness comes in. Sure, during the batches where you test for known values and then you also test for unknown values you do come across some Randomness but it's not true Randomness. During closed testing, you give the neural network access to variables that are now completely out of your control. Before, you could choose where the data was coming from and what the data pertaining to regardless of whether you knew of what the output would be or not.

Beta Testing

Beta testing is when you finally throw complete randomness at your neural network. During the initial testing you are just making sure that it works, and it works well. During closed testing you're creating redundancy at a small scale and during beta testing you're creating that redundancy on a grand scale. Beta testing is the hardest part of any program, regardless of whether it's a neural network or a software, because of the different case scenarios that the programmers simply could not account for because they have a very limited scope of possible scenarios.

Production

Production is the final stage of any particular program that's being developed at any given time. Production refers to the fact that the idea or concept is now within the products phase or the phase in which the company who invested in the venture is now able to make money off of it. It is during this time that the impact of the neural network can be measured over a given time span in the audience that it is designed for.

Expansion

Finally, if this was a hobby then you might not reach this stage but if it's a business than you ultimately want to reach this stage. The expansion stage is where you start the process all over again but instead of starting out with nothing but an idea, you are now finding areas where that idea can further increase its influence. The way that you find this out is you begin looking at the statistical variables gathered from the production cycle, which these will then tell you where your strong points are in the software and you can either make safe bets by finding a way to improve those points or you can take venture risks by investing in the weak spots so that you can flush those out.

Finally, We Come to A Close

Machine Learning with Python is Not Easy

Machine learning is a very hot subject right now and if it seems confusing at this point, it doesn't get any better. As much as one can try to explain it to another individual, machine learning is not a technique, it is not a school of math, it is a mathematical and programming concept that merges several different worlds of sciences together. You have the science of literature for text based neural networks, you have image recognition that takes in the photography and digital design sciences, and you have the predictive sciences that generally make up the rest of what machine learning is about. At first, it's going to seem like you're wading into a pool of mathematics that seem like they are everywhere at once because machine learning is a hot topic that a lot of people try to dumb down so that people get excited about it. The problem is that this doesn't do anyone any favors because machine learning is a complex mathematical art. It requires a significant understanding of statistics, calculus, programming, and conceptual analysis in order to effectively put it into place.

If you are a person who wanted to jump into machine learning because it sounded fun and cool, I completely understand. I see advertisements all the time about how one can go take a course and learn machine learning, but what they don't tell you in that courses that they only teach a very specific type of machine learning for a very specific type of application. Essentially, you have the people who understand what's going on taking advantage of the ignorance of the people who do not understand what's going on. This is why it can seem very confusing to navigate the academic and mathematical literature surrounding machine learning in the first place. That isn't to say that you can't create a neural network in the first year that you go about trying to learn how to perform machine learning, but it is exceedingly rare to create a commercially applicable program within the first year of attempting to learn the science of machine learning itself, especially if you don't feel that you don't have the mathematical capacity that such a science requires of its developer.

Machine Learning with Python is Easy

Having said that, you can easily learn how to program in Python very quickly and there are enough resources that a dedicated individual can learn how to program for machine learning rather quickly. Python has the necessary libraries in order to do this and there are enough companies behind this era of technology that you don't necessarily need the best of computers in order to do the work that you want to do. In fact, depending on how you want to go about doing this you don't actually need to learn how to program your own neural network because some of the companies have actually released API libraries that allow you to use an existing neural network without having to have the hardware.

That means that creating a neural network is easier than ever before and learning how to code a machine learning algorithm inside of python is also the easiest it has ever been. In this book, we have gone over all of the topics I've listed here in the conclusion and I've expanded a little bit further because this is such a vast topic that I want to give you as much information as I possibly can. Having said that, there is a lot more to learn about machine learning than the algorithms that I have listed here, how you can go about developing and deploying a machine learning algorithm, and how to find a profitable algorithm at that. The subject material may be intimidating but just keep in mind that the Python Community is there to back you when you are having trouble.

www.ingramcontent.com/pod-product-compliance
Lightning Source LLC
LaVergne TN
LVHW050148060326
832904LV00003B/54